# Ketogenic Diet

## The No BS Ketogenic Diet Cookbook for Beginners

Learn the Fundamentals of the Keto Diet – Complete Keto Recipes and Meal Plan

# Copyright Legal Information

# Table of Contents

Baked Spiced Granola 669

Flax Sandwich Buns

Breakfast Quiche

Breakfast Sausage 744

The Low Carb Smoothie 916

Tropical Smoothie 1012

Avocado Smoothie 1059

Pumpkin Smoothie 1100

KETOGENIC DIET LUNCH RECIPES

Caprese Stuffed Chicken

Squid Noodle Pasta      1204

Kebab Chicken

Spicy Chicken Lettuce Wrap 2156

Ginger Chicken

Bacon Burrito 3034

Chicken Chowder

BBQ Pork Salad 2414

Bell peppers stuffed with steak and Pastrami

Buffalo Chicken Tenders 3119

Keto Egg Drop Soup with Baby Spinach

Lemon and Garlic Baked Cod 95

Simple Keto Caprese Salad

Spicy Salmon Tandoori 100

Turkey Stir Fry 111

KETOGENIC DIET DINNER RECIPES

Flatbread Pizza

Keto Lasagna 2483

Turkey Cauliflower Casserole

Slow Cooked Pulled Pork 2781

Shredded Chicken Zucchini Boat

Mini Portobello Pizzas

Keto Meatloaf

Pizza with Sausages

Cheddar Pepper Biscuits

Keto Casserole

Herb Baked Salmon

Chicken and Cottage Cheese in Butter Gravy

Chicken Guadalajara

Coconut Chicken Tenders

KETOGENIC DIET SPREADS & SAUCES

Savory Salmon Spread

Spinach & Cream

Garlicky Cilantro Pesto

Low Carb Barbecue Sauce

Cucumber Sauce 149

Hollandaise Sauce 145

Garlic Butter 141

KETOGENIC DIET DESSERTS

Lemon Cheesecake

White Chocolate Raspberry Cheesecake

Coconut Cream Macaroons

Caramel chocolate chip muffin

14 Day Meal Plan

Conclusion

# Introduction

Thank you for purchasing *Ketogenic Diet: The No BS Ketogenic Diet Cookbook For Beginners.*

A ketogenic diet can provide a person with numerous health and medical benefits. One of the best things to keep in mind is why you're doing this. Are you looking to get healthier in general or do you have a specific medical need? With this in mind, you can start to develop a healthier lifestyle, a healthier diet plan, and a healthier you overall.

This diet isn't about deprivation, it's about changing unhealthy patterns and creating a new, healthier lifestyle. Food should provide you with essential building blocks that are needed for making you have a healthier approach on life. The Keto Diet is based on a simple concept. A high intake of naturally fatty food and low intake of carbohydrates is the basis of this diet. You will learn about the whole diet, the benefits that it has to offer, a complete list of recipes, and even tips and answers to FAQs.

This is one of the easiest diets out there to start and to maintain. A ketogenic diet is able to provide you with a lot more nutrients than what you would consider with any other diet, and it involves a lot less work.

This book is designed to help you on your journey for a new lifestyle. You can find not only recipes for the ketogenic diet, but helpful tips and tricks as well. There are guides and appendixes designed to help maintain variety, and thus, your interest in maintaining a new diet plan – as well as meal planning suggestions and templates. With these tools in your arsenal, I hope this book will be able to be your guide and partner in maintaining a healthy lifestyle.

All you need is two weeks to get into a normal Ketogenic Diet routine and then you're able to create great eating habits.

Good luck on this journey and we hope that you find our information useful and helpful on the journey you're going on. You should see some results after you read our book thoroughly and follow our meal plan.

# What is a Ketogenic Diet?

A ketogenic diet is not one of the popular diets that you've heard of. Ketogenic diet considered one of the easiest diets to stick to and helps boost the way you feel. The diet is popularly known as the Keto Diet. It is basically a low carb, high fat diet.

The diet consists of high fat, medium protein and low carbohydrates. The ketones that your liver produces are used as the primary energy source and thus the name of the diet. When you consume carbs, they are broken down into glucose by insulin. The body tends to use glucose over other sources of energy because it is the easiest source to covert. This means that other potential sources, such as fat, are stored in your cells.

When you take out the carbohydrates in your diet, your body will be forced into ketosis. Ketosis is the process where the body shifts from burning glucose to burning fats for energy. At this point, Ketones are used as the main source of energy.

The primary goal of the Ketogenic Diet is to induce your body into a state of ketosis. This environment is created by reducing the intake of carbohydrates.

Since fat is the main source of fuel in the Ketogenic diet, your calorie requirement will be about 70% fat, 25% from proteins, and less than 5% from carbohydrates.

Using Ketosis, your body burns fat instead of the glucose produced by carbohydrates. This causes it to have more fuel to burn throughout the day so you're able to have more energy than before. It is also one of the best ways to shed the fat and lose the pounds.

The fat in the body is converted into fatty acids that are used within the liver. They are then passed through the body as ketones that can be used as glucose sugar, instead of artificial sugars. This helps the body grow and repair itself easily. It is also something that provides the body with enough calories to burn throughout the day without going over them.

Since the Ketogenic Diet is a low carb diet, that means you have to restrict your carb intake. Many of us are used to consuming carbs daily as a staple. For example, rice, spaghetti, pasta, bread are all carbs! Our goal is to make substitute for carbs. For instance, instead of noodles, we will make use of zucchini ribbons or use almond flour pasta.  It may sound difficult at the beginning, but once you rewire your brain to your new habits, losing weight will become fun and enjoyable!

### Regarding Cholesterol:

You don't need to worry about your cholesterol level shooting up. You'll learn about good and bad types of cholesterol. Your body will need some time to get accustomed to the ketogenic diet, so give it some patience. It is advised to keep your exercising schedule on the lighter side during the first ten days of this diet.

# History of Ketogenic Diet

The Ketogenic diet was originally designed in 1920 for children with epilepsy. It was believed that when the ketone passed through the brain and replaced sugar as energy, it would reduce the amount of seizures a child would have.

It was considered a therapeutic diet that was specialized for children with pediatric epilepsy. It provided enough protein for the body to grow and repair itself, but only enough so they were meeting milestones in their growth for their age. The main point of the diet is to eat foods that are high in fat but low in carbohydrates.

As more drugs came out to control epilepsy, the ketogenic diet decreased in popularity. The first time that the public heard about it was in the 1990's when a celebrity had a child with severe epilepsy that was controlled by this diet.

Since the inception of this diet, studies have shown that almost half the people that have tried this diet has had seizures reduce by at least half. Even after the diet ends, the seizures do not come back.

Since the 1990's, the diet has become mainstream. After scientists realized that this diet did not only benefit children, but adults as well, the ketogenic diet has become something that most people are familiar with for weight loss and a healthier lifestyle.

# Ketosis - The Benefits of the Ketogenic Diet

When the body is in a state of ketosis, you're able to use the fats that you put in as fuel. If those fats go unused, they lead to an increase in weight. The use of fats provides the body with the energy that is needed when it comes to burning something other than carbohydrates. The body is more efficient at burning fats instead of carbohydrates, providing it with more energy.

Ketones are something that can be excreted through waste when they are no longer needed. This means that the body is not storing them as fat throughout the body, causing you to gain more weight. Ketones will spare the protein in the body, allowing you to hold onto it and use it wisely. It is also something that can be used when it comes to using the ketones instead of the glucose that the body would normally have to use.

One of the biggest and best benefits that people find when on this diet is that the ketones seem to keep people fuller than the other diets that they have tried in the past.

Hormones that can be stunted throughout the body are released more when it comes to being in a state of ketosis. This allows the body to better utilize the ketones and not have to worry about being too high in the glucose levels that cause diabetes in some people.

By being in a ketone state, it actually turns off your need to eat, thus effectively reducing your appetite significantly. This reduction is automatic. Although you do not have the appetite, it does not mean that you do not eat at all. When it is just protein and fats that you are eating, it makes you fuller quicker.

Placing your body in a ketone state has been shown to be one of the most effective ways to lose weight as you no longer retain as much water. Because of the loss in water weight you become later, combined with the ketone diet, it is very effective for up to half a year before you start to gain weight again. However, most of the weight gained again is because you have changed your diet to something less healthy.

Once you start the ketone diet, you will realize it becomes your lifestyle. A healthier and better lifestyle without giving up most of the foods that you enjoy eating.

With this diet, you will notice that most of the fat that is being reduced will come from your abdomen area. As most people tend to have the most amount of issues with losing weight in the tummy region, it comes as an added bonus with the ketogenic diet. The abdominal region is also the home of many harmful fats. By using this diet, it will help eliminate those harmful fats and reduce heart disease and type 2 diabetes.

The ketogenic diet will also increase your good cholesterol. This will also help in reducing the chances of heart disease. Both blood pressure and sugar levels go down. This leads to a positive change in diabetes and lowers the risk of kidney failure. As this diet requires a lesser amount of carbohydrates, it also removes the issues associated with eating them.

A great benefit is that you lose your sugar cravings and your body will only tell you hungry when it is really hungry and not merely craving for something unhealthy.

When you start the diet, you will find that your body will adjust to it. It will be able to provide you with the energy sources that you need, and ensure that you do not overeat. When you're able to follow along with this diet, you're then able to better your overall health. This is one of the easiest diets out there.

# How the Ketogenic Diet Works

The Ketogenic Diet works by keeping your body running off the fats that you eat throughout the day. It uses fewer carbohydrates that are generally used for energy.

This means that you have to choose certain foods that are going to provide you with this balance of nutrition that is required. You will see a complete list of foods that you can and cannot eat during this diet in the next chapter.

Once you find this healthy balance between the right food and your body, you will be able to start seeing the benefits it has on your body. More Fat will be burnt, since carbohydrates are no longer needed. Though carbohydrates are in almost everything that you eat, you can reduce the amount that you take in, forcing your body to use the fat to run itself.

This provides a way to boost your energy and to boost how you feel. Diets do not have to be difficult. It is important though, to be able to read the dietary facts on the foods that you eat. It is there, that you are going to find out more about the carbohydrates and fats contained in the foods you are consuming.

In order to be successful, you also have to make sure that you stick to the diet. You will need to focus yourself for at least two weeks on this diet before you will see any significant changes to your body.

It is important to remember that once you start, use your willpower to stick to what is prescribed here. There are no cheat days as there is no extreme deprivation of food in this diet. You will have more than enough to eat. It's the matter of what's more important: your health or the taste of your food. Once you see the changes that this diet does to your body, it'll be hard for you to go back to your unhealthy habits!

This diet was basically made for beginners. It is a diet that is easy to do and ensures that you're getting the right nutrition throughout the process.

Certain people may experience a lack of vitamins and minerals; so supplements may be needed to give your body an extra boost.

Should you decide to take supplements, please consult your physician to see if the supplements are compatible with the Ketogenic Diet.

# Foods Do & Don't

This chapter is to provide you with a list of foods that you should and shouldn't eat with this diet. This is a keto friendly guide.

## Eat Freely

**Proteins:**

- Grass fed meats (Beef, goat, lamb)
- Wild caught fish
- Pastured pork, poultry, eggs
- Gelatin

**Non-starchy vegetables:**

- Lettuce, Chives, Bok Choy, Spinach and other green leafy vegetables
- Cruciferous vegetables like kale & radish
- Water rich vegetables like Zucchini, spaghetti squash, celery and cucumbers

**Healthy Fats:**

- Saturated fats – chicken, duck, lard, goose, butter, coconut oil
- Monounsaturated fats – avocado, olive oil, macadamia
- Polyunsaturated fats from animal sources – fatty fish or other seafood rich in Omega-3

**Beverages and condiments:**

- Water, black coffee, green tea, black tea, herbal tea
- Bone broth
- Mayonnaise
- Mustard
- Pickles and fermented foods
- Sauerkraut
- All spices and herbs
- Organic Whey protein

# Eat Occasionally

**Dairy Products:**

- Full fat cream, cheese, or yogurt

**Seeds and Nuts:**

- Macadamia nuts
- Pecans, almonds, sunflower seeds, pine nuts, pumpkin seeds, sesame seeds, etc.
- Brazilian nuts
- Fermented soy products
- Pistachios, cashew nuts, chestnuts
- All non-GMO and soy products like soy sauce and black soybeans

**Vegetables & Fruits:**

- Cruciferous vegetables like cabbage, cauliflower, turnip, Brussel sprouts, and broccoli
- Eggplant, tomatoes, peppers
- Root vegetables like spring onion, garlic, mushrooms, pumpkins, leeks, carrots, beets, and parsnip
- Okra, Snap peas, wax beans, water chestnuts and artichokes
- Raspberries, blackberries, cranberries, strawberries, etc.
- Melons – watermelons, honeydew melon, cantaloupe
- Fruits – apricots, peaches, apples, kiwis, oranges, plums, cherries, pears, etc.

**Condiments:**

- Tomato products without add sugars
- Thickeners like arrowroot powder
- Extra dark chocolate – more than 70% cocoa

- Alcohol – red and white wines and unsweetened spirits (avoid completely if weight loss is your main goal)

# Avoid Eating

**Carbohydrates:**

- Avoid ALL grains – no pasta, breads, pizzas, rye, whole wheat, barley, millets, etc.
- Quinoa, white potatoes, corn
- Use almond flour to substitute for regular flour

**Factory Meats:**

- Farmed in factory pork and fish (Rich in Omega-6 fatty acids)

**Processed Foods:**
- Sugary and sweet treats – soft drinks, ice cream, sugary syrups, cakes
- Products that contain MSG, wheat glutens and dried fruit
- Refined fats, oils and trans fats like margarine, sunflower oil, canola oil, corn oil, grapeseed oil
- "low fat", "Low carb" products – they contain artificial additives

**Tropical Fruits:**

- Pineapple, mangoes, bananas, papayas, tangerine, grapes
- Fruit juices
- Some of these fruits contain high carb count, additives, and unnecessary sugars.

# Ketogenic Macros: What is it?

Macros tracking is an important part of the Ketogenic Diet. However, when we hear tracking, we think about advanced excel sheets and daily commitment to stare at the nutritional ingredients of everything we eat. To ease any fears, I can say that Ketogenic Macros tracking can be easy and doesn't have to be complicated. Let me give a simple explanation of what exactly macros are first.

The term "macros" is short for Macronutrients. Macronutrients are the energy-giving components of food that fuels our body. Carbohydrates, protein and fat are the three main types of nutrients that your body burns for energy. In the Ketogenic Diet, the goal is to reduce the amount of carbs you intake and to take your body to ketosis. This will in turn make your body into a fat burning machine!

**About Carbohydrates**

The reason why the Ketogenic Diet works is because our bodies does not require carbohydrates for survival. Carbohydrates are made up of sugar and starches, and this is what we need to cut out of our diet. In the Keto Diet, we are allowed a total "Net Carb" amount per day. This is the carb limit allowable in our diet. This calculation is done by having your **Total Carbs – Fiber = Net Carbs.**

In order to successfully reduce your carb intake, we will need to identity what foods are low in carbohydrates and which ones to avoid. It is best to check your nutritional labels, and plan your meal plan around the low carb ingredients. In our case for starters, we want to have a **daily intake of 20 grams of net carb.**

**Carbohydrates provide 4 calories per gram. Therefore 4 calories x 20 grams of net carb = 80 calories per day.**

**About Protein**

One other part of the puzzle is protein. Protein is important for growth, immune functions, making essential hormones and enzymes, and preserving lean muscles. Protein is an essential building block for our body. A deficiency in protein or any essential amino acids can result in malnutrition and other health complications.

In the Ketogenic diet, our goal is to have enough protein in our system to maintain your lean body mass/muscles. A reasonable standard that we will follow is this: **0.8 to 0.9 grams of protein per pound of muscle to maintain standards.**

Though many of you want to lose weight, it's best to keep in mind that you don't want to lose the MUSCLE MASS you currently have. The goal is to lose the extra FAT and to preserve the muscles. It's important to shift your mindset from weight loss to fat loss.

This is an example of how to calculate your daily protein calorie intake:

You are 180 pounds with 30% body fat percentage.

Therefore you are approximately 54 pounds of body fat and 126 pounds lean body mass

126 pounds lean muscle x 0.8 grams of protein = 100.8 grams of protein

**Protein is 4 calories per gram**

4 calories x 100.8 of protein = 403.2 calories from protein daily

**About Fat**

Fat is critical for growth and development, and also for absorbing vitamins. They also provide a protective cushion for our organs and bones. The best part is that they help us feel full and adds flavor to the food we eat!

**Fats provide 9 calories per gram.**

You may think, isn't it counter intuitive to eat more fats in our system? Especially when we are trying to get rid of fat?

The problem is we need fat to survive. The Ketogenic Diet is to drive your body in the BURNING fat, so that the fat doesn't stick around. You will still need to eat enough calories from fat to support your total daily energy expenditure. This is dependent on your metabolic rate and also your exercise rates. The more you burn, the more you have to eat.

## Example of Calculating Macros

All this may seem difficult to understand, but below is an example of the entire calculation. You can do the calculation manually, but I would recommend you to use a simple keto calculator such as https://www.ruled.me/keto-calculator/ or https://keto-calculator.ankerl.com/

Paul is a 6'2", 180 pound male in his 30s. He has 30% body fat and doesn't work out at the gym. His goal is to lose fat.

According to the calculator at https://www.ruled.me/keto-calculator/

He needs to take in 1506 calories, which includes 114 g fats, 20 g of carbs, and 101 g protein

= 1026 calories of fat, 80 calories of carbs, 404 calories of protein

= 68% fats, 5% carbs, 27% protein

This will give Paul a good idea of how many grams and calories he needs to input in order to lose weight. This is the macros that he needs to aim for with his daily diet.

# Ketogenic Diet Frequency Asked Questions (FAQ)

**Q: Is it necessary to count calories?**

Calories matter in the Ketogenic Diet. Simply put, the more calories you put in, the more weight you will gain. However, don't cut out all your food and stop eating! You will need to eat properly and make sure that your body doesn't have a severe deficit of calories. If you feel hungry, eat healthy snacks as necessary that are allowed within the diet. Our included meal plan generally gives you enough calories to get you through your day. As for the question, there is no 100% proven answer. It is best to use counting calorie as a tool to help you track your food intake. Once track, you will have a rough estimate of what you're putting in and gauge the amount of food you should or should not eat.

**Q: How long does it take for ketosis to set in?**

A: You must be consistent with the keto diet. It will take your body some time to get adjusted and for ketosis to set in. This process can take anywhere between four to seven days. It is dependent on the level of activity, your body type, and the food that you are eating. If you start exercising on an empty stomach, this will help in inducing ketosis rather quickly. Start restricting your carb consumption to less than 20g per day to speed up the process.

**Q: What about eating too much fat?**

A: That's a possibility. Use an app to keep track of your food intake. It is best to follow the meal plan in order to keep yourself on track.

**Q: What about low/no carb recipes? Can I use those?**

A: The goal of this diet is low to no carbs. We have over 50 recipes in this book that fulfill the Ketogenic Diet requirement. If you find other ones, you are more than welcome to use it! Just remember that it's important to know what you can and cannot eat. It's good to experiment and making your own meals based on those foods.

**Q: How do I track the intake of carbs?**

A: There are various paid and free mobile apps that you can make use of for tracking your carb intake. They can help you track your total carb and fiber intake. However you won't be able to track your net carb intake. MyFitnessPal is one of the popular apps.

**Q: What would the weight loss look like?**

A: This is a very personalized question. The diet will cause you to lose a lot of your excess water weight and get you to ketosis, where you will burn fat rather than glucose. Your weight loss will depend on how much water weight you have originally, and how fast your body gets you to ketosis. Also, exercising will help you significantly in your weight loss journey. If you exercise regularly, try increasing the intensity of your exercise. High intensity interval training or circuit training can boost your weight loss to the next level.

**Q:** How can you tell if your body is in ketosis?

A: The most common way to tell if your body is in ketosis is to use Ketostix. These are found in local pharmacies. However, Ketostix have been known to be inaccurate. Ketostix help measure the level of acetone present in your urine. If you want an accurate measure of the ketone levels in your body, then make use of a blood ketone meter. These will show you the actual number of ketones present in your bloodstream and it isn't influenced by your hydration levels. The blood ketone meter should be the following:

- Light ketosis: between 0.5-0.9 mmol/L
- Medium ketosis: between 0.9-1.4mmol/L
- Deep ketosis: between 1.5-3.0mmol/L

**Q:** Should I worry about all the fat I am consuming?

The fats that are being consumed are categorized into three main groups. They are saturated fats, polyunsaturated fats, and monounsaturated fats. Saturated fats help you with improving your level of cholesterol, so these are not a major concern. Dealing with the polyunsaturated fats is your biggest concern. Products like margarine and vegetable oil consist of this type of fat, so they are best to be avoided. The last type of fat, the monounsaturated fats, are considered healthy, such as olive oil.

**Q:** What can be done if you feel a little low during the initial phase of the diet?

A: During the initial phases of the ketogenic diet, you may experience mild headaches and feel low on energy. Ketosis will also increase the urge to urinate more than usual. With electrolytes being pushed out of your body, you will need to replace them more often. The solution is to keep yourself fully hydrated. Add salt to your food. Consume broth and lots of water. You will make your life a lot better by staying consistently hydrated.

**Q:** What can be done if I experience constipation?

A: Help yourself to some magnesium supplements, drink lots of water, and drink a tablespoon of coconut oil.

**Q:** Is alcohol permitted?

A: Yes! Alcohol is permitted, but be mindful about what you are consuming. There are carbs in the barley in beer, and watch out for sweeteners in many liquors. Stick with red or white wine or clear liquor.

**Q:** What can be done if you stop losing weight?

A: Hitting a plateau in your weight loss is a common thing. Here's a few things that you can try to induce the weight loss again:

- Cut down on dairy
- Increase fat intake
- Decrease carb intake
- Stop consuming nuts
- Cut out gluten
- Increase the intensity of your exercises

# KETOGENIC DIET BREAKFAST RECIPES

Breakfast is a hectic time. The kids are getting up, you or your spouse is ready to leave for work, there's a lot going on.  Though many of us believe that breakfast is the most important meal of the day, we often don't have a chance to eat it!

When we selected our breakfast recipes, we picked one that were easy to make. Most of these recipes can be made in under ten minutes. We also put in some smoothie recipes to ensure that you don't miss your meal even if you're in a huge rush. We've kept it simple and quick for your day to day needs. We did put in a couple of recipes that takes time to make for your weekend meals. These breakfasts can be a treat to yourself and your family!

# Cream Cheese Pancake

**COOK TIME**
15 MIN
**SERVINGS**
4 SERVINGS

## INGREDIENTS

- 2 ounces of cream cheese
- 2 large eggs
- 1 tablespoon sugar substitute
- 1 tablespoon roller oats
- ½ teaspoon cinnamon
- Strawberries for garnish
- Butter

## PREPARATION

1. In a large bowl, beat the cream cheese until it is nice and fluffy

2. Crack the eggs one by one and beat the mixture altogether

3. Lightly crush the oats using a pounder

4. Drizzle in sugar substitute, cinnamon powder and gently fold the mixture in

5. Grease a saucepan with oil or butter to heat over a medium flame

6. Add one scoop of batter and spread it across the pan, cook the pancake for 2 minutes until it turns golden brown. Flip to cook for another minute. Repeat process for remaining batter

7. Transfer to a dish and chop strawberries to add to the top of the pancake. Serve warm.

# Cinnamon Apple Muffins

**COOK TIME**
40 MIN
**SERVINGS**
6 SERVINGS

## INGREDIENTS

### For the muffins:
- ½ cup coconut flour
- 6 eggs
- 4 tablespoons flaxseed powder
- 1 apple, peeled, cored, diced
- 10 walnuts, chopped
- 1 cup plain yogurt
- 4 tablespoons almond milk
- ½ cup sugar free maple syrup

- ½ teaspoon soda
- ½ teaspoon salt
- 4 teaspoons ground cinnamon

### For the glaze:
- 4 tablespoons butter, melted
- ½ cup sugar free maple syrup
- 4 teaspoons ground cinnamon

## PREPARATION

1. To make muffins: Mix together all the dry ingredients in a bowl, including the diced apple.

2. Mix together all the wet ingredients in a bowl. Add the dry ingredients to the wet ingredients and whisk well.

3. Pour into greased muffin cups ¾ of the way and bake in a preheated oven at 350 F for about 20-30 minutes or until it turns light brown.

4. Remove from the oven and set aside to cool for about 10 minutes. Meanwhile, mix together the ingredients of the glaze.

5. Loosen the edges with a knife. Invert on to a plate and brush with the glaze. Serve warm.

# Ketogenic Pancakes

**COOK TIME**
10 MIN
**SERVINGS**
2-4 SERVINGS

## INGREDIENTS

- ½ cup all-purpose flour
- 1 cup breakfast oats
- 2 tablespoons flax seeds
- 1 teaspoon baking soda
- ¼ teaspoon salt

- 2 cups Greek yogurt
- 2 large eggs
- 2 tablespoons honey
- 2 tablespoons canola oil
- Toppings – fresh berries

## PREPARATION

1. Grind oats into a coarse powder in a mixer or a stone grinder – add it to a bowl. Then use a sieve to sift in the flour and baking soda into the bowl, combine and mix well. Add the salt and mix well.

2. Mix the yogurt, eggs, honey and vanilla and the olive oil together, beat until well combined.

3. Make a small well in the center of your mixed dry ingredients then pour the liquid into it. Mix well until everything is combined and forms a smooth batter.

4. Place a griddle on medium-high heat drizzle a little bit of olive oil. Once it's heated, pour a ladleful of the batter to make a thick pancake.

5. Allow it to brown on one side before flipping to brown the other side. Repeat the process until you run out of batter.

6. Serve hot with a drizzle of honey and fresh fruits on top.

# Ketogenic Waffles

**COOK TIME**
10 MIN
**SERVINGS**
2 SERVINGS

## INGREDIENTS

- 5 eggs
- 5 tablespoon coconut flour
- 3 tablespoon sugar substitute
- 4 tablespoon chocolate shavings
- 1/4 teaspoon baking soda
- 1 tablespoon vanilla essence

## PREPARATION

1. Mix flour & baking soda in a large bowl

2. In another bowl, crack open the eggs and beat them while adding the vanilla essence

3. Pour the liquid ingredients into the other bowl and continue to whisk

4. Heat the waffle maker over medium heat

5. Pour one scoop of the battle on the waffle maker, cook for 5 minutes on each side until golden brown

6. Transfer the waffles onto a plate, sprinkle chocolate shaving and serve warm

# Breakfast Muffins

**COOK TIME**
30 MIN
**SERVINGS**
6 SERVINGS

## INGREDIENTS

- 2 cups Almond Flour
- ½ cup cheddar
- ½ cup mozzarella
- ½ teaspoon dried thyme
- ½ baking soda
- Pinch of salt
- 1 cup sour cream
- 2 eggs
- 1/8 square butter (melted)

## PREPARATION

1. Oven preheat to 400 F. Whisk together all dry ingredients. In another bowl, lightly beat eggs. Mix in sour cream and butter with the eggs until smooth. Mix both bowls until smooth. Add cheese.

2. Pour muffin tin about half full. Bake for 15-20 minutes. It's ready when you stick a toothpick in and it comes out clean. Serve with side of fresh fruits and Greek yogurt.

# Dark Chocolate Sour Cream Muffin

**COOK TIME**
30 MIN
**SERVINGS**
6 SERVINGS

## INGREDIENTS

- 2 cups Almond Flour
- ½ teaspoon baking soda
- Pinch of salt
- 1 cup sour cream
- 2 eggs
- 1/8 square butter (melted)
- ½ cup dark chocolate chips

## PREPARATION

1. Oven preheat to 350 F. Whisk together all dry ingredients. In another bowl, lightly beat eggs. Mix in sour cream and butter with the eggs until smooth. Mix both bowls until smooth. Add dark chocolate chips. Pour muffin tin about half full.

2. Bake for 20 minutes. It's ready when you stick a toothpick in and it comes out clean. Serve with side of fresh fruits and Greek yogurt.

# Italian Omelet

**COOK TIME**
20 MIN
**SERVINGS**
4 SERVINGS

## INGREDIENTS

- 6 eggs
- ½ cup full fat Brie cheese, sliced
- 3 tablespoons butter
- 15 kalamata olives, pitted
- 3 tablespoons MCT oil
- 1/2 teaspoon salt
- 1 1/2 teaspoons Herbes De Provence
- 1 large avocado, peeled, pitted, cut into thick slices

## PREPARATION

1. Add eggs, oil, herbes de Provence, olives and salt. Whisk well. Place a nonstick skillet over medium - high heat. Add butter. When the butter melts, add avocado and fry until golden brown all over. Remove and set aside.

2. Place the skillet back on high heat. Add the egg mixture into it. Place the cheese slice on the egg. Cover and cook until the underside is golden brown. Flip sides and cook the other side too. Remove from the pan. Slice into 6 wedges. Top with avocado slices and serve.

# Baked Eggs

**COOK TIME**
5 MIN
**SERVINGS**
1 SERVING

## INGREDIENTS

- 2 large pasteurized egg, beaten
- ¼ cup spinach
- Pink Himalayan salt to taste
- 2 slices, Crispy pastured bacon

## PREPARATION

1. Preheat oven to 375 F. Mix together all the ingredients and place in an oven-proof ramekin.

2. Bake in middle rack of hot oven for 10 to 15 minutes or until the eggs are solid and a golden yellow.

3. Serve hot with a side of fresh orange juice.

# Mini Santé Fe Frittata's

**COOK TIME**
30 MIN
**SERVINGS**
4 SERVINGS

## INGREDIENTS

- 5 large eggs
- 1 egg white
- ½ cup pork sausage
- ¼ cup milk
- ½ cup red bell pepper, coarsely chopped in small cubes
- ½ cup yellow bell pepper, coarsely chopped in small cubes
- ¼ cup pepper Jack cheese
- Salt to taste
- Pepper powder to taste
- 1 onion, sliced
- 2 tablespoons fresh cilantro, chopped

## PREPARATION

1. Preheat oven to 350 F.

2. Place a skillet over medium heat. Add the sausages and cook until done. Remove with a slotted spoon and set aside. Wipe off excess fat and place the skillet back on heat. Add peppers and cook until tender. Remove from heat and set aside.

3. Add eggs, egg white and milk to a bowl and whisk well. Take 6 muffin cups and grease it with a little butter or oil. Add bacon to the cups. Next layer with bell peppers. Pour the egg mixture on top and top with shredded cheese. Stir lightly with a fork.

4. Bake for about 20-30 minutes or until it browns. Remove from the oven. Let cool for a few minutes before loosening the edges with a knife. Invert on to a plate and serve.

# Tomato Broccoli Frittata

**COOK TIME**
40 MIN
**SERVINGS**
4 SERVINGS

## INGREDIENTS

- 5 eggs, whisked
- 1 tablespoon olive oil
- 1 ounce Gouda cheese, crumbled
- 1 small head broccoli, chopped into small florets

- 1 medium tomato, chopped
- ½ teaspoon pepper powder
- 1 small avocado, peeled, pitted, sliced

## PREPARATION

1. Preheat the oven to 425 F.

2. Add eggs, broccoli, tomato, salt and pepper to a bowl and whisk to combine. Add cheese and stir to incorporate. Place an ovenproof pan over medium heat. Add oil to the pan and swirl the pan so that the oil spreads evenly.

3. Add the egg mixture and cook until the sides are slightly set. Remove from heat.

4. Bake for about 20-30 minutes or until golden brown. Slice and serve with avocado slices.

# Egg Benedict

**COOK TIME**
50 MIN
**SERVINGS**
4-6 SERVINGS

## INGREDIENTS

### For protein bun:
- 6 eggs, separated
- 1 teaspoon fresh dill or any other fresh herb of your choice
- ½ cup unflavored egg white protein

### For toppings:
- 24 large eggs
- 24 slices ham

### For hollandaise:
- 4 tablespoons Dijon mustard
- 12 large egg yolks
- 3 cups melted butter, unsalted
- Freshly ground black pepper
- ½ teaspoon cayenne pepper
- 1 teaspoon salt
- ½ cup lemon juice

## PREPARATION

1. To make the buns: Beat the egg whites until stiff peaks. Add protein powder, dill, and the yolks. Fold gently. Pour or spoon mixture into a lightly greased muffin pan.

2. Bake in a preheated oven at 325 F for about 20-30 minutes or until golden brown. Remove from the oven and cool completely.

3. To make the hollandaise sauce: Add yolks, lemon juice and mustard to a heatproof bowl. Place the bowl in a double boiler. Whisk until well blended.

4. Pour the melted butter in a thin drizzle (very slowly) whisking simultaneously. Add salt, pepper and cayenne pepper whisking simultaneously until thick. Taste and adjust the seasonings if necessary. Remove from the double boiler and set aside.

5. For toppings: Bring a pot of water to boil and add 3-4 table spoons of vinegar. Gently crack 1 or 2 eggs at a time into the water and cook until the egg whites are solid, approximately 3-4 minutes. Remove the eggs with a slotted spoon and set aside.

6. To serve: Slice a protein bun in half and place on a plate. Lay a slice of ham on top of each slice, followed by a poached egg. Spoon 2-3 tablespoons of hollandaise sauce on the eggs.

7. Serve immediately.

# Baked Spiced Granola

**COOK TIME**
90 MIN
**SERVINGS**
2-4 SERVINGS

---

## INGREDIENTS

*For protein bun:*
- 8 tablespoons chopped pecans
- 4 tablespoons chopped walnuts
- 4 tablespoons almonds
- 4 tablespoons unsweetened coconut flakes
- 4 tablespoons almond meal
- 2 tablespoons flax meal
- 2 tablespoons pumpkin seeds
- 2 tablespoons sunflower seeds

- Melt butter
- 4 tablespoons sugar substitute
- 1 teaspoon honey
- 1 teaspoon cinnamon powder
- 1 teaspoon vanilla
- ½ teaspoon nutmeg
- ½ teaspoon salt
- ½ cup water

---

## PREPARATION

1. Preheat the oven to 340 F.

2. Combine all the nuts with flax meal, pumpkin seeds, sunflower seeds, sugar substitute, honey, ground cinnamon, nutmeg, salt, almond meal, coconut flakes and mix well

3. Drizzle melted butter on top along the almond meal to fold it in

4. Place parchment paper on the baking tray

5. Transfer the granola tray and place another sheet of parchment paper on the granola. Use a rolling pin to even it out

6. Place the tray in the oven to bake for 80 minutes until brown and crisp. Let cool for 30 minutes and store in airtight container.

7. Suggestion: Mix the granola with almond milk for breakfast

# Flax Sandwich Buns

**COOK TIME**
30 MIN
**SERVINGS**
4 SERVINGS

## INGREDIENTS

- 9 tablespoons flaxseed meal
- 1 teaspoon caraway seeds
- 2 teaspoons onion powder
- 3 large eggs
- 1 teaspoon baking powder
- 1 ½ tablespoons water
- 2 drops Stevia
- 1 ½ tablespoons olive oil

## PREPARATION

1. Preheat the oven to 325 F and lightly grease a muffin pan.

2. Mix together all the dry ingredients in a bowl. And mix together all the wet ingredients in another.

3. Pour the wet ingredients into the bowl of dry ingredients and mix well. Fill the muffin pan about 2/3 of the way. Bake for about 15 minutes or until it done. Slice each bun in the middle, horizontally, and serve with toppings of your choice.

# Breakfast Quiche

**COOK TIME**
30 MIN
**SERVINGS**
6 SERVINGS

## INGREDIENTS

- 6 cups shredded cheddar cheese
- Butter
- 1 red onion
- 12 eggs

- 2 cups cream (heavy)
- 1 teaspoon salt
- 2 teaspoon thyme

## PREPARATION

1. Preheat the oven to 350 F. and lightly grease a baking dish. Melt butter in skillet and sauté onions until translucent.

2. Whisk eggs, cream and spices together until bubbly. Add the onions and cheese to the baking dish and pour the egg mixture on top. Bake for 25 minutes or until set. Serve with fresh juice on the side.

# Breakfast Sausage

**COOK TIME**
30 MIN
**SERVINGS**
4-6 SERVINGS

## INGREDIENTS

- 1 large red bell pepper
- 1 large green bell pepper
- 1 teaspoon olive oil
- 1 teaspoon spike seasoning
- ¼ teaspoon ground black pepper
- 12 sausages
- 4 tablespoons grated mozzarella cheese

## PREPARATION

1. Preheat oven to 430 C

2. Grease a baking dish with cooking spray

3. Wash the bell peppers under running water and pat them dry. Dice them with a kitchen knife

4. Place bell peppers at the bottom of the baking dish. Drizzle olive oil and sprinkle seasoning, ground black pepper, and place the tray inside the oven

5. Bake the dish for 20 minutes

6. While baking, heat a saucepan over medium heat and add sausages. Brown them from all sides for about 10-15 minutes.

7. Transfer the sausages on to a cutting board and slice them to small pieces

8. Once the peppers are baked, add sausage slices along with grated cheese, bake for 5 more minutes. Serve hot

# The Low Carb Smoothie

**COOK TIME**
5 MIN
**SERVINGS**
4-6 SERVINGS

---

## INGREDIENTS

- 4 cups water
- 2 teaspoons chopped pineapple
- ¼ head romaine lettuce
- 2 tablespoon fresh parsley

- Half a cucumber, peeled and chopped
- ½ cup kiwi fruit, peeled and sliced
- ½ slice avocado
- Ice cubes

---

## PREPARATION

1. Wash the lettuce and chop them up with a kitchen knife

2. Add lettuce to the blender, add remaining ingredients in as well

3. Give ingredients in the blender a whisk, use blender to blend the mixture into a smooth paste (about 1-2 minutes)

4. Pour smoothie into a glass and serve with ice cubes

# Tropical Smoothie

**COOK TIME**
15 MIN
**SERVINGS**
4-6 SERVINGS

---

## INGREDIENTS

- 1 cup coconut milk
- ¼ cup sour cream
- 2 tablespoon flaxseed meal
- ½ teaspoon mango essence
- ¼ teaspoon banana essence
- Ice cubes

---

## PREPARATION

1. Add flax seed meal to coconut milk and let soak for 10 minutes

2. Add remaining ingredients to the mixture. Put into blender and whisk until smooth and lump free. (about 1-2 minutes)

3. Pour into glass and add ice cubes, serve chilled

# Avocado Smoothie

**COOK TIME**
10 MIN
**SERVINGS**
4-6 SERVINGS

---

## INGREDIENTS

- 1 ¼ cup almond milk
- ½ cup whipping cream
- 1 medium sized avocado
- ½ teaspoon vanilla essence
- Ice cubes

---

## PREPARATION

1. Wash with water and peel the skin of the avocado using a knife

2. Add avocado to the blender along with other ingredients, blend until smooth and lump free (about 1-2 minutes)

3. Pour into glass and add ice cubes, serve chilled

# Pumpkin Smoothie

**COOK TIME**
10 MIN
**SERVINGS**
4-6 SERVINGS

## INGREDIENTS

- 1/3 cup pumpkin puree, homemade or canned
- ¼ cup almond milk
- ½ cup coconut milk
- ½ teaspoon pumpkin pie spice powder
- 1 tablespoon extra-virgin coconut oil
- 2 tablespoons whipped cream
- Ice cubes

## PREPARATION

1. Combine all the ingredients together and add to blender. Blend for 2-3 minutes on high until you get a smooth, lump free mixture

2. Pour into glass and add ice cubes, serve chilled

# KETOGENIC DIET LUNCH RECIPES

Lunch time often involves something simple to make and quick to eat. Lunches are designed to keep us going until dinner time, but many of us feel the "afternoon slump" after we eat a heavy meal. In our selection of Keto lunches, we picked many lighter recipes, including salads, wraps, and soups to help you get through your weekdays. We didn't forget to put in some bigger serving meals in there for your weekend lunch plans!

# Caprese Stuffed Chicken

**COOK TIME**
1 HOUR 10 MIN
**SERVINGS**
4 SERVINGS

## INGREDIENTS

- 4 boneless and skinless chicken breast
- ½ bottle garlic and herb marinade
- 2 tomatoes, sliced
- 4 slices mozzarella cheese
- 12 slices of bacon
- 12 fresh basil leaves

## PREPARATION

1. Place the chicken breast onto a clean cutting board and slice a little pocket along the long side of the chicken breast. Try not to cut through to the other side.

2. Place the cut chicken breast in a large bowl and pour the marinade over the chicken. Make sure to rub some marinade into the cut area. Set aside to marinate for 30 minutes.

3. Preheat oven to 400 F and grease a baking dish

4. Arrange the marinated chicken into pan and stuff the chicken with the sliced tomatoes, mozzarella and fresh basil leaves.

5. Seal the pocket by threading a skewer or tooth pick over the cut edge. Wrap 3-4 slices of bacon around each chicken breast.

6. Bake for 20 minutes and then flip the chicken breast over and bake for an additional 15 more minutes or until the chicken is fully cooked.

# Squid Noodle Pasta

**COOK TIME**
30 MIN
**SERVINGS**
4 SERVINGS

## INGREDIENTS

- 4 boneless and skinless chicken breast
- ½ bottle garlic and herb marinade
- 2 tomatoes, sliced

- 4 slices mozzarella cheese
- 12 slices of bacon
- 12 fresh basil leaves

## PREPARATION

7. Place the chicken breast onto a clean cutting board and slice a little pocket along the long side of the chicken breast. Try not to cut through to the other side.

8. Place the cut chicken breast in a large bowl and pour the marinade over the chicken. Make sure to rub some marinade into the cut area. Set aside to marinate for 30 minutes.

9. Preheat oven to 400 F and grease a baking dish

10. Arrange the marinated chicken into pan and stuff the chicken with the sliced tomatoes, mozzarella and fresh basil leaves.

11. Seal the pocket by threading a skewer or tooth pick over the cut edge. Wrap 3-4 slices of bacon around each chicken breast.

12. Bake for 20 minutes and then flip the chicken breast over and bake for an additional 15 more minutes or until the chicken is fully cooked.

# Kebab Chicken

**COOK TIME**
30 MIN
**SERVINGS**
4 SERVINGS

---

## INGREDIENTS

- 4 boneless and skinless chicken breasts
- 6 jalapeno peppers, seeds removed and chopped
- ¼ cup raw almonds
- 8 cloves of garlic
- 1 cup fresh cilantro, roughly chopped
- Pinch of salt
- Juice of one lemon

---

## PREPARATION

1. Cut the chicken breast into 1 ½ inch pieces and place in a large bowl.

2. In a blender, blend the almonds, jalapeno peppers, garlic, and cilantro until smooth. Pour in the lemon juice and a pinch of pepper. Blend until combined.

3. Pour the mixture over the chicken and set aside to marinate for about ten minutes.

4. Meanwhile, soak a handful of bamboo skewers in a bowl of water to soften and prevent it from burning on the grill.

5. Skewer the chicken, about 4 chunks per skewer. Season with a pinch of salt or to taste.

6. Grill chicken skewers on medium high heat, turning each skewer over occasionally, until chicken is fully cooked. Serve over herbed cauliflower rice.

# Spicy Chicken Lettuce Wrap

**COOK TIME**
30 MIN
**SERVINGS**
4 SERVINGS

## INGREDIENTS

- 4 small chicken breasts
- 1 cup grape tomatoes
- 2 tablespoon red chili paste
- 1 teaspoon smoked paprika
- 2 tablespoon lemon juice
- 1 small avocado

- 4 large iceberg lettuce leaves
- 2 tablespoon Dijon mustard
- 4 tablespoon sour cream
- ½ teaspoon salt
- ¼ teaspoon pepper
- 1 tablespoon olive oil or butter

## PREPARATION

1. Clean the chicken breasts properly and dry using paper towels. Trim off the excess fat

2. Add water to a large pot and bring to boil. Insert the chicken and cover the lid. Cook the chicken until it is pink. Once complete, remove the chicken onto the cutting board and slice up into chunks

3. Combine salt, pepper, chili pasta, paprika and lemon juice and mix well. Coat the chicken with this mixture and place in refrigerator for 20 minutes. Remove from the fridge to allow it to come to room temperature

4. In a bowl, combine the Dijon mustard and sour cream and mix well. Add chicken chunks and toss

5. Wash the lettuce leaves and dry them, fill the leaves with the chicken mixture. Wrap the lettuce leaves and secure with toothpick.

6. Serve warm with optional hot sauce

# Ginger Chicken

**COOK TIME**
20 MIN
**SERVINGS**
2 SERVINGS

## INGREDIENTS

- 2 chicken breast
- 1 tablespoon olive oil
- 1 red onion (diced)
- 1 clove of garlic (diced)

- 1 slice ginger root
- 1/2 lemon, cut into wedges
- Salt
- Pepper

## PREPARATION

1. Cut chicken into strips 1 ½ inch thick. Place oil in skillet over high heat. Place chicken into skillet. Reduce heat. Cook for 5 minutes.

2. Add onion and garlic. Add ginger, salt and pepper. Over and simmer for 5 minutes. Squeeze lemon juice over top before serving.

# Bacon Burrito

**COOK TIME**
15 MIN
**SERVINGS**
2 SERVINGS

## INGREDIENTS

- 4 cups raw Spanish
- ½ cup chopped shallots
- 6 slices bacon

- 2 tortillas
- 1 tablespoon butter

## PREPARATION

1. Slice the bacon strips and melt butter on the skillet on medium heat

2. Add the shallots and the bacon to the skillet. Sauté until shallots have turned golden brown

3. Add spinach to the skillet and cook until leaves have wilted, mix all the skillet ingredients together

4. Transfer this mixture onto the tortilla and roll to serve

5. Optional: add mayonnaise sauce

# Chicken Chowder

**COOK TIME**
30 MIN
**SERVINGS**
4 SERVINGS

---

## INGREDIENTS

- 1 cup coconut milk
- 1 ½ cups pound chicken
- 1 cup pound beef
- 3 cups vegetable stock
- 1 ½ cups cauliflower florets
- 1 cup chopped carrots
- ½ teaspoon. ground coriander
- ½ cup chopped celery
- ½ cup diced onions
- 1 tablespoon. chopped dill
- 1 teaspoon. sliced garlic
- 1 teaspoon. ground cinnamon
- ½ teaspoon. turmeric powder
- 1 tablespoon. olive oil
- Salt and pepper as per taste

---

## PREPARATION

1. Heat a pan on medium heat and add oil. When the oil is hot, sauté the onions until golden brown. Lightly cook the chicken and beef.

2. Reduce the heat and add the vegetables to the pan. Sauté for a few minutes.

3. Pour in the stock and simmer on medium heat until the vegetables are tender, meat is fully cooked, and the stock has thickened.

4. Garnish the chowder with dill and serve hot.

# BBQ Pork Salad

**COOK TIME**
10 MIN
**SERVINGS**
4 SERVINGS

## INGREDIENTS

### For the salad
- ½ pound cooked pulled pork
- ½ cup chopped cilantro
- 1 head romaine lettuce
- 1 chopped red bell pepper

### For the BBQ Sauce
- 4 tablespoon tomato paste
- 2 teaspoon creamy peanut butter
- 1 lime
- 2 teaspoon red curry paste
- ½ teaspoon red pepper flakes
- 5-6 tablespoon soy sauce or coconut amino
- 2 teaspoon five spice powder
- 3 tablespoon rice wine vinegar
- 2 teaspoon fish sauce

## PREPARATION

1. To make sauce: whisk together all the sauce ingredients in a bowl and set aside

2. To make the salad: mix together the lettuce, cilantro, and red bell peppers in a bowl

3. Divide the salad into 4 plates, place the pork on top and pour sauce to serve

# Bell peppers stuffed with steak and Pastrami

**COOK TIME**
20 MIN
**SERVINGS**
2 SERVINGS

## INGREDIENTS

- 1 tablespoon onion, chopped
- 1 tablespoon ghee or olive oil
- A pinch of rosemary
- ½ pound shaved beef steak
- ¼ pound red pastrami, cut into 1 inch pieces
- 2 green bell peppers, tops removed, de-seeded
- ½ tablespoon prepared mustard
- 1 ½ tablespoon mayonnaise
- 2 slices cheese

## PREPARATION

1. Preheat the oven to 350 F.

2. Melt ghee, or heat up the olive oil, in a frying pan on medium heat.

3. Add onions and sauté until the onions are translucent. Add the rosemary, steak, a pinch of salt and pepper and cook until the steak is browned.

4. Add the pastrami and cook until fragrant.

5. Remove from heat and add the mustard and mayonnaise. Place bell peppers on a baking tray in a preheated oven at 350 F and bake for 2-3 minutes. Remove.

6. Fill the bell peppers with the steak mixture. Top with a slice of cheese.

7. Bake for 2-3 minutes until the cheese is melted. Serve hot.

# Buffalo Chicken Tenders

**COOK TIME**
40 MIN
**SERVINGS**
4 SERVINGS

## INGREDIENTS

- 1 pound chicken breast tenders
- ½ cup almond flour
- 1 egg
- 2 tablespoon heavy cream

- 1 cup buffalo sauce
- ½ teaspoon kosher salt
- ½ teaspoon black pepper

## PREPARATION

1. Preheat the oven to 180 C

2. Grease a baking pan with cooking spray

3. Clean the chicken tenders, season them with salt and pepper and set aside for 15 minutes

4. Spread almond flour on a dish

5. In a bowl, crack the egg and combine it with heavy cream

6. Dip the chicken tenders in the egg mixture first and then into the almond flour. Place them one by one on the baking dish and set it inside the oven

7. Bake for 30 minutes until golden brown. Broil them if you want them crispier

# Keto Egg Drop Soup with Baby Spinach

**COOK TIME**
10 MIN
**SERVINGS**
2 SERVINGS

## INGREDIENTS

- 3 cups chicken broth (you can use either homemade or low sodium store bought broth)
- 1 teaspoon sesame oil
- 2 large eggs
- 1 teaspoon chili garlic paste
- 1 cup packed, baby spinach leaves

## PREPARATION

1. In a medium sized non-stick soup pot, over medium heat, bring to a boil the 3 cups chicken broth.

2. While it is boiling. In a small mixing bowl, quickly whisk the eggs with the garlic paste and sesame oil.

3. Slowly pour the egg mixture into the chicken broth, let it sit for a moment, then stir. Add in the spinach leaves and stir. Let it boil for about 1 minute and its ready to be served.

4. Pair this soup with your favorite sushi or smoked salmon salad.

# Lemon and Garlic Baked Cod

**COOK TIME**
30 MIN
**SERVINGS**
2 SERVINGS

## INGREDIENTS

- 2-3 pounds cod fillets
- 5 tablespoons extra virgin olive oil
- 1 ½ tablespoon lemon juice
- 2 garlic cloves
- Salt and pepper

## PREPARATION

1. Preheat oven to 200 C and grease an oven tray

2. Place cod fillets on the dish and drizzle with olive oil

3. Crush garlic and spread over fillets

4. Place into oven and bake for 20 minutes until cooked, serve hot

# Simple Keto Caprese Salad

**COOK TIME**
10 MIN
**SERVINGS**
2 SERVINGS

## INGREDIENTS

- 1 large beef steak tomato
- 1 cup fresh mozzarella cheese
- ½ cup fresh basil leaves

- 3 tablespoon olive oil
- 1 tablespoon balsamic vinegar
- Fresh cracked pepper and sea salt to serve

## PREPARATION

1. In a food processor or blender, pulse the basil leaves with the olive oil several times to make a paste.

2. Cut the tomato into slices, you should get about 6 slices. Slice the mozzarella in the same way and begin layering your Caprese salad.

3. Place a tomato slice on to a plate and spread some basil paste over it.

4. Add a slice of mozzarella and a thin spread of basil paste on top as well. Continue this layering process three more times.

5. Spoon any leftover basil paste on top. Serve with fresh cracked pepper and sea salt and a small drizzle of olive oil and balsamic vinegar.

# Spicy Salmon Tandoori

**COOK TIME**
30 MIN
**SERVINGS**
2 SERVINGS

## INGREDIENTS

- 1.5 pounds salmon in pieces
- 2 tablespoon tandoori seasoning
- 3 tablespoon coconut oil

## PREPARATION

1. Preheat oven to 175 C and grease an oven pan

2. In a small bowl, mix the tandoori seasoning with the oil and stir well.

3. Place fish onto the oven dish, pour tandoori seasoning mixture onto the fish until coated

4. Place the salmon into the oven for 20 minutes, serve hot

# Turkey Stir Fry

**COOK TIME**
30 MIN
**SERVINGS**
2 SERVINGS

## INGREDIENTS

- 1 tablespoon coconut oil or olive oil
- 1 tablespoon sesame oil
- 2 minced garlic cloves
- 2 tablespoons minced ginger
- 1 pound ground turkey
- 1 pound Asian vegetable mix (broccoli, Brussel sprouts, etc.)
- 4 tablespoon low sodium soy sauce
- 2 tablespoon rice vinegar

## PREPARATION

1. Gently warm the oils in a frying pan or wok on medium heat.
2. Add the turkey, garlic and ginger and let it cook for 5 minutes
3. Add the veggies and let it cook for 5 more minutes until tender
4. Add the soy sauce and vinegar and cook for another 2-3 minutes until turkey is cooked, serve hot

# KETOGENIC DIET DINNER RECIPES

Dinner time is always a good time. It's finally the end of the day and you can relax a bit, and make yourself and your family a bigger meal. We've saved the best meals for last. We have recipes on chicken, seafood, and carb alternative pizza and pastas. Most of these recipes take a bit longer to make, but these delicious meals are well worth your time spent!

# Flatbread Pizza

**COOK TIME**
15 MIN
**SERVINGS**
2 SERVINGS

---

## INGREDIENTS

*For the crust:*
- 2 cups part-skim mozzarella cheese, grated
- ¾ cup almond flour
- 2 tablespoon cream cheese
- ½ teaspoon. sea salt
- 1/8 teaspoon dried oregano
- 1 cup pepper jack cheese, grated
- ½ small red onion, cut into thin slices
- 1 medium sized red bell pepper, seeded and cored, sliced into strips
- ½ cup Low carbohydrate sliced ham, cut into chunks
- 1/8 teaspoon dried thyme
- Salt and Pepper to taste

---

## PREPARATION

1. Preheat oven to 425 F. Cut two pieces of parchment paper about 2 inches larger than a 12-inch pizza pan. Have a rolling pin and a 12-inch pizza pan ready.

2. In a double boiler, partially fill one pot with water. Over high heat, bring water in the pot to a simmer, then turn heat to low.

3. In the mixing bowl for the double boiler, add mozzarella cheese, cream cheese, almond flour, thyme and salt. Place the bowl over the simmering pot and stir constantly. When the cheese melts enough, that the ingredients hold together and starts to resemble dough, take it off the heat and dump it onto one of the prepared pieces of parchment. Knead a few minutes to mix dough thoroughly.

4. Roll the dough into a ball, then place onto the center of the parchment paper. Pat into a disk shape and cover with the other piece of parchment. Using the rolling pin, gently roll the dough into a 12-inch circle.

5. Place the dough and the bottom piece of parchment onto the pizza pan. Using a fork, poke holes all over the dough. Place pan in oven and bake for about 6-8 minutes, watching carefully. Remove when it is golden brown. Decrease the oven setting to 350 F.

6. Sprinkle ¼ cup of the cheese over the flatbread.

7. Arrange onion slices, bell peppers and ham. Then layer with the remaining cheese and sprinkle thyme and salt and pepper. Bake in middle rack at 350 F until cheese is melted and golden brown, about 7 minutes. Serve immediately with fresh green salad.

# Keto Lasagna

**COOK TIME**
40-50 MIN
**SERVINGS**
4 SERVINGS

## INGREDIENTS

- 1 pound Italian sausages
- ¾ pound ground beef
- ½ yellow onion, sliced
- 1 teaspoon minced garlic
- 1.5 ounce marinara sauce
- 1 pound ricotta cheese

- 1 egg
- ½ teaspoon salt
- ¾ pounds sliced mozzarella cheese
- 2 1/2 ounces shredded Parmesan cheese
- 1 pound boneless chicken breast

## PREPARATION

1. Preheat the oven to 430 F and grease a baking tray using cooking oil or butter

2. Slice up the Italian sausages into small pieces

3. Add them to a bowl with the ground beef, onion, marinara sauce, garlic and mix well.

4. Heat the saucepan over medium flame to add the sauce. Cook for 5 minutes on low flame until it starts to thicken

5. In the meantime, add ricotta cheese to a bowl with salt. Crack open the egg into the bowl and mix well

6. Pat dry the chicken breast and trim off excess fat

7. Place the chicken breast slices on the baking dish and pour the beef sauce on top

8. Spread the ricotta cheese mixture on top and spread evenly

9. Add Parmesan cheese and repeat the layers of cheese one by one

10. Cover the baking dish with a foil but do not let it touch the lasagna

11. Bake in the oven for 30 minutes until the cheese is golden brown

12. Allow it to cool for 15 minutes and serve hot

# Turkey Cauliflower Casserole

**COOK TIME**
40-50 MIN
**SERVINGS**
4 SERVINGS

## INGREDIENTS

*Turkey meat seasoning*
- 1 pound ground turkey meat
- 1 tablespoon sesame oil
- 1 tablespoon minced garlic
- 1 teaspoon oregano
- 1 teaspoon thyme
- 1 teaspoon onion powder
- 1 teaspoon light soy sauce

- ½ teaspoon sea salt
- 
- 1 medium sized Cauliflower head, rinsed and cut into florets
- ½ cup light cream cheese
- ½ cup shredded pepper jack cheese
- ½ cup fresh chopped parsley leaves for garnish

## PREPARATION

1. In a large mixing bowl mix the turkey meat with all the seasonings. Set aside.

2. Preheat oven to 350 F. In a non-stick ovenproof casserole dish, lay out your Cauliflower florets and set aside.

3. In a non-stick frying pan, brown your turkey mixture over medium heat for 15 minutes. Use a wooden spoon to break up the large chunks (it does not have to be fully cooked) then evenly spread the turkey meat over your cauliflower along with the cream cheese and shredded jack cheese.

4. Bake in middle rack, for 40 minutes, until all the cheese is completely melted and browned. Garnish with the fresh parsley leaves and with a side of fresh cucumber salad.

# Slow Cooked Pulled Pork

**COOK TIME**
4 HOURS
**SERVINGS**
4 SERVINGS

## INGREDIENTS

- 3.5 pounds pork shoulder
- 2 sliced onions
- 4 minced garlic cloves
- 1 cup Chicken stock
- ½ cup keto friendly BBQ sauce
- 1 tablespoon chili powder
- 1 teaspoon salt
- ½ teaspoon paprika
- ½ teaspoon garlic powder
- ½ teaspoon ground black pepper
- ½ teaspoon cumin
- 1 tablespoon olive oil

## PREPARATION

1. Combine all the dry ingredients in a bowl and mix them together

2. Trim off the excess fat off the pork shoulders. Pat dry and brush them with olive oil.

3. Coat the pork shoulders with the dry ingredient mixture

4. Heat the slow cooker on medium heat, lay the onion slices at the bottom of the cooker

5. Place in the pork shoulder and sprinkle minced garlic on top

6. Pour your chicken stock and BBQ sauce on top and close the cooker

7. Let cook for 8 hours on low or 4 hours on high

8. Once complete, move the pork shoulder onto a plate or bowl. Shred the pork and drizzle the remaining sauce on top

9. Serve hot

# Shredded Chicken Zucchini Boat

**COOK TIME**
40 MIN
**SERVINGS**
4 SERVINGS

---

## INGREDIENTS

- 2 large zucchini cut in half, hallowed out with a spoon (keep the flesh in a separate bowl)
- 1 tablespoon melted butter
- ½ cup shredded sharp cheddar
- 1 cup raw chicken breast, sliced thinly
- ½ teaspoon sea salt
- ½ teaspoon white pepper
- ½ teaspoon dried parsley flakes
- ½ teaspoon oregano
- ½ tablespoon low fat sour cream
- 1 teaspoon sesame oil
- 1 stalk green scallion, thinly sliced

---

## PREPARATION

10. Preheat oven to 400 F. Lay out your zucchini boats on a non-stick baking sheet and set aside.

11. In a small mixing bowl combine the chicken breast with sea salt, white pepper, parsley flakes, and oregano and sesame oil. Set aside.

12. Heat up a small non-stick frying pan with the butter, sauté the chicken breasts until the meat turns golden brown about 10-15 minutes. Then set aside.

13. In another mixing bowl, combine the spooned out zucchini flesh with the scallions and sour cream. Then add in the cooked chicken breast. Mix well.

14. Evenly distribute the chicken mixture between your zucchini boats, and then bake in middle rack for 20 minutes. Once time is up take it out and sprinkle the cheese over the boats and bake again for another 10-15 minutes, until the cheese is melted and golden brown. Serve immediately with fresh cracked pepper and a glass of fresh fruit infused water or smoothie.

# Mini Portobello Pizzas

**COOK TIME**
10-15 MIN
**SERVINGS**
2 SERVINGS

## INGREDIENTS

- 6 large Portobello mushroom caps
- 1 medium vine tomato, sliced into 6 slices
- ½ cup shredded mozzarella cheese
- ½ cup chopped basil leaves

- 4 tablespoon olive oil
- 30 slices of pepperoni
- Fresh cracked pepper and sea salt to serve

## PREPARATION

1. Wash and cut of the stem of each Portobello mushroom.

2. Rub each cap, inside and outside with olive oil, pepper and sea salt, then lay caps facing down onto a baking sheet and broil at 500 F in middle rack for 5 minutes. Repeat this step with the caps facing up.

3. Remove from oven and put a slice of tomato in each cap, then 5 slices of pepperoni and dis-tribute the basil leaves and shredded mozzarella evenly between the 6 Portobello mushroom caps.

4. Place the assembled caps into middle rack and broil again for another 5 minutes or until cheese is melted and starting to brown.

5. Serve with fresh greens and fresh smoothie.

# Keto Meatloaf

**COOK TIME**
1 HOUR
**SERVINGS**
6 SERVINGS

## INGREDIENTS

- 4 teaspoon. Dijon mustard
- 2 pound Italian sausage
- 4 tablespoon butter for sautéing
- 4 pounds 85% ground beef
- 1 cup almond flour
- 2 tablespoon. thyme leaves*
- ½ cup minced fresh parsley leaves*
- 1 cup shredded Parmesan cheese (not dry grated)
- 4 T Low Carb Barbecue sauce
- ½ cup heavy cream
- ¼ cup of cream cheese
- 4 eggs
- 2 tablespoon fresh basil leaves, chopped fine*
- 4 cups shredded cheddar cheese
- 2 cups chopped green pepper
- ½ cup chopped white onion
- 2 teaspoon. salt
- ¼ teaspoon. unflavored gelatin
- 1 teaspoon. ground black pepper
- 8 garlic cloves, minced

## PREPARATION

1. Preheat the oven to 300 F. In a small bowl add the Parmesan cheese and almond flour and mix well. In another bowl and add the cream cheese and the cheddar cheese and mix until smooth.

2. Heat a saucepan over a medium heat. Once hot, add oil and sauté the onion, garlic and pepper. Cook until onions are translucent and soft. Set aside to cool. When cool, blend it in a food processor. In another small bowl, whisk the eggs and spices. Season with salt, pepper and the barbecue sauce. When incorporated, add the cream and stir. When mixed well, sprinkle the gelatin and let it set for ten minutes.

3. Meanwhile, finely chop the beef and Italian sausage. If the mixture is too sticky, add the Parmesan cheese, one spoon at a time. Knead until soft. Add the egg mixture to the meat and stir in the rest of the ingredients. Add the flour one spoon at a time and continue to mix until ingredients come together.

4. Spread the meat mixture on a greased baking dish lined with parchment paper and allow it to rest for 10 minutes. Spread the cheese mixture on top of the meat. When the meat is covered, use the parchment paper to roll up the meat. Do not roll the paper in the meat.

5. Seal the ends of the meat roll. Bake for 15 minutes. Ensure that the meat is well cooked. You can do so by inserting a food thermometer in the meat, the meat has to be 300 degrees F. Let it cool when done. Serve your favorite sauce.

# Pizza with Sausages

**COOK TIME**
1 HOUR 30 MIN
**SERVINGS**
2 SERVINGS

## INGREDIENTS

- 1 tablespoon. olive oil
- 1/2 cauliflower head (trim and then chop the head into smaller pieces)
- ½ ounce white onion (minced)
- 2 tablespoon. butter
- ½ cup water
- 2 eggs
- 2 cups mozzarella cheese (shredded and chopped into smaller pieces)
- 1 teaspoon. fennel seeds
- 2 teaspoon. Italian seasoning
- ¼ cup Parmesan (grated)
- 3 ounces Pizza Sauce (any sauce that is low in carbs)
- ½ pound Italian sausage (any kind that is low amount of carbs)
- ½ cup Italian cheese (try to get the 5-cheese blend - shredded)

## PREPARATION

### For the crust

1. Preheat the oven to 400 F. Grease a large baking sheet. Melt butter in a medium skillet on medium heat. Sauté onions until translucent. Toss in the cauliflower and sauté. Add some water and cover with a lid, cook until vegetables are soft. Once done, set aside to cool.

2. Once the cauliflower mix has cooled down, take 2 cups and blend until smooth. In a large mixing bowl, add eggs, Parmesan cheese and the spices to the mixing bowl and mix well.

3. Spread a circle of the cauliflower puree on the greased baking sheet. Make sure not to make too thin of a layer – about 1 1/2 inches in thickness. Bake the crust in the oven for 15 minutes. As the crust turns brown on the edge, remove it from the oven.

### For the pizza

1. Set the oven to broil. Remove the sausage casings and break the sausage into smaller pieces. Sauté in a dry skillet. When done, drain the excess fat. Let the sausages cool.

2. In a large sauce pan, pour in the pizza sauce. Add half of the cook sausage and bring the sauce to a boil. To assemble the pizza, pour the pizza sauce over the cauliflower crust. Add your toppings and sprinkle cheese on top.

3. Broil option till the cheese melts. When the cheese starts to bubble, remove the pizza from the oven. Cut it into slices and serve hot.

# Cheddar Pepper Biscuits

**COOK TIME**
1 HOUR 30 MIN
**SERVINGS**
2 SERVINGS

## INGREDIENTS

- 10 cups almond flour
- 8 large eggs
- 24 ounces Colby jack cheese (shredded)
- 32 ounces cream cheese
- 20 tablespoon. butter, room temperature
- 4 teaspoon. baking soda
- 8 teaspoon. ground pepper
- 3 teaspoon. sea salt

## PREPARATION

1. Preheat the oven to 300 F. Line or grease a cookie sheet.

2. Blend the cheese and 2 cups of the almond flour in a food processor until mixture is granular. Set aside.

3. In a large mixing bowl, whisk together the cream cheese and butter until smooth.

4. Add eggs and whisk until smooth. Season with salt and pepper, followed by a tablespoon of baking soda, Continue to whisk until mixture is glossy and sleek. Stir in the almond flour and cheese mixture one half at a time until well incorporated. At the end, you should be left with a soft dough.

5. Scoop a tablespoon of the dough onto the cookie sheet and gently pat the dough into a biscuit shape. Make sure to keep about an inch gap between each biscuit.

6. Bake for about 30 minutes until the biscuits have turned golden brown. Once done, let the biscuits cool to room temperature before serving.

# Keto Casserole

**COOK TIME**
30 MIN
**SERVINGS**
2 SERVINGS

## INGREDIENTS

- ½ pound corned beef, diced
- ½ can sauerkraut, drained
- 1 cup Swiss cheese, shredded
- ¼ cup homemade mayonnaise
- 4 ounce cream cheese
- ¼ cup low sugar ketchup
- 1 tablespoon pickle brine or ½ teaspoon vinegar
- 1/2 tablespoon salt
- ¼ teaspoon garlic salt
- ¼ teaspoon caraway seeds

## PREPARATION

1. Preheat the oven to 350 F and lightly grease a baking dish.

2. Heat a saucepan over low heat. Add the cream cheese, mayonnaise, and ketchup to it. When melted, add ¾ cup Swiss cheese, sauerkraut and beef.

3. Stir until well combined and the cheese has melted. Remove the pan from heat and add the pickle brine. Mix well. Pour into the greased baking dish.

4. Sprinkle with the remaining cheese and caraway seeds.

5. Bake for around 20 minutes or until the cheese brown and bubbly. Serve hot.

# Herb Baked Salmon

**COOK TIME**
30 MIN
**SERVINGS**
2 SERVINGS

## INGREDIENTS

- 2 large salmon filets
- 1 cup fresh green beans
- 1 cup fresh mushrooms, chopped

*For the marinade:*
- ½ cup tamari soy sauce
- 4 ounces sesame oil
- 1 teaspoon. garlic, minced
- ½ teaspoon. ground ginger

- 1 teaspoon. oregano leaves
- ½ teaspoon. basil
- ½ teaspoon. thyme
- ½ teaspoon. tarragon
- ½ teaspoon. rosemary
- 4 ounces butter
- ½ cup green onions, chopped

## PREPARATION

1. Cut the salmon filets into 1 ½ inch chunks and place it into a large freezer bag. Mix together the sesame oil, soy sauce and the spices. Pour into the freezer bag with the salmon and let it marinate in the fridge for a few hours or overnight.

2. Preheat the oven to 300 F and line a baking dish with aluminum foil, shiny side up.

3. Remove the salmon from of the refrigerator and pour the contents into the center of the baking dish. Place the mushrooms and green beans and mushrooms on both sides of the salmon. Drizzle olive oil over the vegetables and season with salt and pepper to taste.

4. Bake for 20-25 minutes or until the salmon is fully cooked. Serve hot.

# Chicken and Cottage Cheese in Butter Gravy

**COOK TIME**
1 HOUR 30 MIN
**SERVINGS**
2 SERVINGS

## INGREDIENTS

- 1 ½ pounds chicken thighs with bones
- 3 ½ ounce Cottage cheese (fresh cheese), cut into cubes
- ½ cup water
- ½ cup pureed tomatoes
- ¼ cup heavy cream
- 3 tablespoons butter
- ½ tablespoon olive oil
- 1 teaspoon coconut oil
- ¾ teaspoon ginger paste
- ¾ teaspoon garlic paste
- ½ teaspoon coriander, ground
- Salt to taste
- ½ teaspoon garam masala powder (mixed spice powder, can be found in your local Indian store)
- ½ teaspoon black pepper powder
- ½ teaspoon paprika
- ½ teaspoon red chili powder
- Cilantro for garnishing, chopped

## PREPARATION

1. Preheat the oven to 375 F.

2. Rub the chicken thighs with olive oil, a little salt, and pepper. Set aside for 15-20 minutes.

3. Roast in for about 25 minutes or until almost cooked. At this point, remove from the oven and cool. Remove the bones from the chicken pieces and set aside.

4. Place the butter and coconut oil in a medium sized pan over medium heat.

5. When butter melts, add ginger and garlic paste. Sauté for a few minutes. Add the tomatoes, coriander powder, chili powder, garam masala and paprika. Let it simmer for a while until the butter starts showing at the top.

6. Add the Cottage cheese cubes and water and simmer for a few minutes. Add cream and continue simmering. Add the chicken pieces and simmer for another 5 minutes. Sauce is ready when it has reduced and thickened.

7. Serve hot garnished with cilantro leaves.

# Chicken Guadalajara

**COOK TIME**
40 MIN
**SERVINGS**
4 SERVINGS

## INGREDIENTS

- 2 tablespoon. butter
- 4 boneless, skinless, chicken breast halves
- 4 ounces white onions (chopped finely)
- 3 garlics (minced cloves)
- 3 ounces cans of green chilies
- 3 ounces cans diced tomatoes
- ½ cup chicken broth
- ½ cup whipped cream
- ½ teaspoon. cumin (dried)
- ½ teaspoon. garlic powder
- ½ teaspoon. cayenne pepper
- 1 teaspoon. sea salt
- Grated cheddar cheese (as per preference)
- Sour cream (as per preference)
- Salsa (as per preference)

## PREPARATION

1. Clean the chicken breasts, pat them dry and slice into strips. Take a skillet and heat it on a medium heat. Add the butter in the skillet and allow it to melt. Once done, add the onions and garlic to the skillet and let it cook till the onions are soft.

2. Add the chicken to the skillet and sauté until fully cooked. Make sure you drain out the excess fat from the chicken. Lower the heat and toss in the chili and tomatoes in the skillet. Put a lid on the skillet and let it cook it for about fifteen minutes.

3. Then add the cream cheese to the mixture and stir it well till the cheese melts. Once done, add the sour cream and mix well. Ensure that the chicken and the veggies get coated with cheese.

4. Once done, add the broth simmer until mixture has reduced slightly. Top with garnishes and serve hot.

# Coconut Chicken Tenders

**COOK TIME**
25 MIN
**SERVINGS**
4 SERVINGS

## INGREDIENTS

- 1 pound boneless, skinless chicken tenders
- 1 egg
- 1/2 cup cashew flour
- 1 cup unsweetened shredded coconut
- 1/4 teaspoon salt
- 1/4 teaspoon pepper
- 1/4 teaspoon garlic powder
- 1/8 teaspoon of cinnamon

## PREPARATION

1. Preheat oven to 375 degrees.

2. Beat egg in a bowl and set aside.

3. Mix cashew flour, coconut, and spices in another bowl or dish.

4. Dip each chicken tender lightly in the egg and then in the batter.

5. Place the coated chicken tenders on a baking sheet lined with foil or parchment paper.

6. Bake for 15-20 minutes until chicken is fully cooked. Serve with a hearty salad or some French fries on the side.

For a special treat, try deep frying the chicken tenders in some coconut oil for an extra crunch. Make sure to pat off excess oil before digging in!

# KETOGENIC DIET SPREADS & SAUCES

How can we forgot the spreads and sauces to add onto your delicious meals? These spreads are perfect for your healthy snacks, or as an add-on for your meals. These will make good companions for your Ketogenic snacks.

# Savory Salmon Spread

## COOK TIME
5 MIN

## INGREDIENTS

- 8 ounces Cream Cheese
- ½ sour cream
- 1 tablespoon lemon juice
- ½ teaspoon salt
- ¼ teaspoon ground black pepper
- ¼ pound salmon (minced)

## PREPARATION

1. With electric mixer, cream cheese, sour cream, lemon juice, salt and pepper.

2. Add smoked salmon.

3. Fold until mixed well.

4. Chill and serve with crackers.

# Spinach & Cream

## COOK TIME
10 MIN

---

## INGREDIENTS

- 1 bundle spinach
- 1 red onion
- 1 clove garlic minced
- 2 tablespoon butter
- ½ cup heavy cream
- Salt
- Pepper

---

## PREPARATION

1. Melt butter on skillet and saute onion and garlic. When the onions have soften and the garlic is fragrant, add in spinach.

2. Sauté on medium heat. And then let the mixture steam for 5 minutes. Add cream, salt and pepper.

3. Let the mixture simmer for another 5 minutes until the sauce has thickened.

# Garlicky Cilantro Pesto

**COOK TIME**
5 MIN

## INGREDIENTS

- 4 cups cilantro leaves
- 5 cloves garlic (diced)
- Salt
- Pepper
- ½ cup olive oil
- 2/3 cup cashew
- 4 ounces mozzarella cheese

## PREPARATION

1. Put all ingredients in a high power food processor. Pulse until it is texture resembles a pesto.

2. Add salt and pepper to taste.

3. Use as a sandwich spread or with zucchini noodles.

# Low Carb Barbecue Sauce

## COOK TIME
40 MIN

## INGREDIENTS

- 1/2 onion, finely chopped
- 2 tablespoons butter
- 2 teaspoons bacon fat
- 3 cloves garlic, minced
- 15 ounce can tomato sauce
- 1 teaspoon Worcestershire sauce .
- 2 teaspoons liquid smoke, hickory or mesquite flavor
- 1 teaspoon Tabasco sauce
- 1/2 teaspoon gravy flavoring
- 2 tablespoons coconut sugar
- 1/2 cup cider vinegar
- Salt and Pepper to taste

## PREPARATION

1. Sauté the onion and garlic in the butter and bacon fat until soft.

2. Mix in the rest of the ingredients and simmer, uncovered, over low heat for about 30 minutes.

3. If you prefer a smooth sauce, puree the mixture using a food processor or an immersion blender.

4. Makes about 2 cups.

# Cucumber Sauce

**COOK TIME**
5 MIN

## INGREDIENTS

- 1 ¼ cups mayonnaise
- ½ shredded cucumber
- 2 minced garlic cloves
- Juice from ½ lime
- ½ teaspoon salt

## PREPARATION

1. Use a bowl and put all the ingredients together

2. Mix well and enjoy

# Hollandaise Sauce

**COOK TIME**
15 MIN

## INGREDIENTS

- 1 ½ cup unsalted butter
- 3 large egg yolks
- 3 tablespoon water
- 1 tablespoon fresh lemon juice
- Salt and pepper

## PREPARATION

1. Place a wet paper towel into a sieve and place over a saucepan

2. Place the butter in a saucepan and heat over medium heat. Keep the heat until butter clears and the foam falls to the bottom

3. Pour the butter through the sieve and set aside

4. Separate the eggs and water and place into bowl over boiling pan of water and whisk. Add the butter slowly, whisking constantly to combine the mixture

5. Add the lemon juice, salt and pepper and serve

# Garlic Butter

**COOK TIME**
5 MIN

## INGREDIENTS

- 5 ounce butter
- 1 garlic clove
- ½ tablespoon garlic powder
- 4 tablespoon chopped parsley
- 1 teaspoon lemon juice
- Salt and pepper

## PREPARATION

1. Add all ingredients and mix well into a bowl

2. Put mixture into the refrigerator for 30 minutes, then serve

# KETOGENIC DIET DESSERTS

Who can forget the dessert! Just because you're on the Ketogenic Diet doesn't mean you need to skimp out on our favorite meal of the day. Though it is recommended to control you cravings and calorie into, we can still indulge ourselves occasionally in cakes and muffins. The following are some Keto friendly dessert to end your day on a sweet note.

# Lemon Cheesecake

**COOK TIME**
2 HOURS
**SERVINGS**
8 SERVINGS

## INGREDIENTS

- 8 ounces cream cheese
- 2 ounces heavy cream
- 1 teaspoon sugar
- 1 tablespoon lemon juice
- 1 cup sour cream
- 3 dashes vanilla extract

## PREPARATION

1. Blend all ingredients in a blender until smooth. Pour mixture into a 6 inch pie or cake dish.

2. Refrigerate until set.

# White Chocolate Raspberry Cheesecake

**COOK TIME**
2 HOURS
**SERVINGS**
8 SERVINGS

## INGREDIENTS

- 8 ounces cream cheese
- 2 ounces heavy cream
- 1 teaspoon raspberry (mulched)
- 1 tablespoon chocolate syrup
- Chocolate shavings

## PREPARATION

1. Mix everything until smooth.

2. Refrigerate until set.

3. Add chocolate shavings prior to serving.

# Coconut Cream Macaroons

**COOK TIME**
1 HOUR 30 MIN
**SERVINGS**
6 SERVINGS

## INGREDIENTS

- 2 large eggs whites
- ½ teaspoon. vanilla extract
- ¼ teaspoon. cream of tartar
- 1/8 teaspoon. salt
- 1 cup coconut sugar

- 8 ounces unsweetened dried coconut, shredded
- 4 ounces cream cheese (soften at room temperature)
- 1 ounce heavy cream
- 2 ounces chocolate chips

## PREPARATION

1. Preheat the oven to 300 F and line a cookie sheet with parchment paper.

2. In a large mixing bowl, beat the egg whites, cream of tartar and the salt using an electric mixer or by hand with a balloon whisk.

3. Sprinkle in the coconut sugar one tablespoon at a time and beat until the mixture is smooth. Be careful not to over whip the egg whites. Add the coconut and fold well to incorporate it into the egg whites.

4. In a separate mixing bowl, beat the cream cheese and heavy cream until fluffy. Fold in half of the white chocolate chips and vanilla extract.

5. Add the cream cheese mixture to the egg white mixture one third at a time, gently folding to avoid deflating the egg whites. Spoon in 1 tablespoon of the dough onto the cookie sheet.

6. Bake for 30 minutes, and then let the macaroons dry in the oven for an additional 30 minutes. Transfer the macaroons onto a cooling rack when done.

7. Melt the rest of your chocolate chips in 15 second intervals in the microwave until smooth. Drizzle the melted chocolate over the macaroons and let the chocolate harden before serving.

# Caramel chocolate chip muffin

**COOK TIME**
1 HOUR
**SERVINGS**
12 SERVINGS

## INGREDIENTS

- 3 cups almond flour
- ¼ cup raw honey
- 1 teaspoon. baking soda
- 1 teaspoon. salt
- 3 large eggs, lightly beaten
- 1 ½ cup sour cream
- 3 tablespoon. melted butter
- 2 teaspoon. coconut sugar
- 1 cup low carb caramel dip
- 2 cups Chocolate chips

## PREPARATION

1. Preheat the oven to 300 F and line or grease a muffin tray. In a medium bowl, add the almond four, blacking soda, and salt. Mix well.

2. In a separate bowl, beat the eggs with the coconut sugar. Then whisk in the honey, butter, and sour cream until everything is well combined.

3. Pour the egg mixture into the flour mixture and combine. When the batter is smooth and there are no visible lumps of flour, fold in the chocolate chips. Fill each muffin cup ¾ of the way and drizzle a little bit of caramel into the batter – do not stir.

4. Bake for 30 minutes until the muffins are golden brown and a toothpick comes out clean. Remove the muffins from the oven and let it cool for about 10 minutes in the pan. This will make it easier to remove the muffins.

5. When cool, store the muffins in an airtight container in the refrigerator for up to 5 days.

# 14 Day Meal Plan

Meal planning can be very easy after only a couple of weeks of trying recipes and reading about this diet. You will quickly see what is included and what can be eaten in moderation. Soon enough, it will be intuitive for you in determining what to buy, make and consume.

Start by thinking in broad strokes about the foods that you have a full green light to consume, those that can be consumed but to a lesser degree (yellow light) and those to avoid (red light). Remember to refer to our "Foods Do and Don't" Chapter earlier in the book. This is a short summary of that list.

**Green light**: Proteins (Red meats), Non starchy vegetables, Healthy Fats, water, coffee, and tea

**Yellow light**: Dairy Products, Seeds and Nuts, Cruciferous and Root Vegetables, some condiments, Alcohol

**Red light**:  Carbohydrates, Factory Meats, Processed Foods

If you would prefer to think about the diet in terms of a time line, consider the foods you can aim to eat daily and those that should be reserved for a weekly or monthly schedule. Daily you can focus your consumption on proteins and vegetables. Weekly would mean an indulgence once or twice a week, but not daily. For example, dairy products or seed and nuts as snacks. Lastly, any unhealthy processed foods or carbohydrates should be consumed once a month or so, and if you can help it, even less frequently. Treat yourself to a cheat meal of spaghetti or a bag of chips.

That should help you define the main principles. Selecting recipes from the previous chapters can make the learning curve quite painless as well, and certainly fun. You can select from breakfasts, mains, salads, snacks and you can even find recipes for desserts if you have a sweet tooth (of course sugar is always used in moderation in this lifestyle).

In terms of what to drink, make water your primary beverage when on the Ketogenic Diet. Many are pleased to find that this diet also includes moderate amounts of red wine. Two to three glasses a week is considered reasonable. This matches with the social component of this lifestyle. Picture people gathered around the kitchen, cooking and sipping wine. You also have the green light for coffee and teas, so this will work when you are out for work meetings or for social gatherings.

Below is a full, comprehensive sample meal plan guide for you while you are getting started in this lifestyle.

## Week 1

### Monday

Breakfast: Egg Benedict

Lunch: Kebab Chicken

Dinner: Keto Lasagna

### Tuesday

Breakfast: Italian Omelet

Lunch: Spicy Chicken Lettuce Wrap

Dinner: Turkey Stir Fry

### Wednesday

Breakfast: Breakfast Muffins

Lunch: BBQ Pork Salad

Dinner: Herb Baked Salmon

### Thursday

Breakfast: Keto Pancakes

Lunch: Bacon Burrito

Dinner: Keto Casserole

**Friday**

Breakfast: Breakfast Sausage

Lunch: Chicken Chowder

Dinner: Mini Portobello Pizzas

**Saturday**

Breakfast: Avocado Smoothie

Lunch: Simple Keto Caprese Salad

Dinner: Coconut Chicken Tenders

**Sunday**

Breakfast: Tomato Broccoli Frittata

Lunch: Lemon and Garlic Baked Cod

Dinner: Flatbread pizza

# Week 2

**Monday**

Breakfast: Tropical Smoothie

Lunch: Squid Noodle Pasta

Dinner: Chicken Guadalajara

## Tuesday

Breakfast: Flax Sandwich Buns

Lunch: Chicken Chowder

Dinner: Cheddar Pepper Biscuits

## Wednesday

Breakfast: Breakfast Quiche

Lunch: Spicy Salmon Tandoori

Dinner: Caprese Stuffed Chicken

## Thursday

Breakfast: Low Carb Smoothie

Lunch: Keto Egg Drop Soup with Baby Spinach

Dinner: Keto Meatloaf

## Friday

Breakfast: Mini Sante Fe Frittatas

Lunch: Bell peppers stuffed with steak and Pastrami

Dinner: Pizza with Sausage

**Saturday**

Breakfast: Egg Benedict

Lunch: Herb Baked Salmon

Dinner: Keto Casserole

**Sunday**

Breakfast: Dark Chocolate Sour Cream Muffin

Lunch: Turkey Stir Fry

Dinner: Coconut Chicken Tenders

When you plan your shopping trips, think about spending the majority of time in the produce area. Vegetables and meats are the foundation of the diet. Go for lots of different colors and be sure to stock up on leafy greens and pick up your fresh meats. Your next priority is dairy and fruits, so make sure you have everything for your smoothie mornings. Don't forget to pick up the spices and oils required for your recipes.

There is a great deal of flexibility with this diet as you can see. This means that you can substitute seafood for fresh meats or spinach for lettuce. You have the ability to cater to you and your families likes and dislikes easily. If you observe the essence of this diet, you will quickly make it your own and establish your favorite recipes while still leaving yourself lots of room to experiment.

# Conclusion

The Ketogenic Diet is a great one for beginners. As it is easy to do and requires much less dedication and understanding of what kind of food should be going into your body. It does not stop you from eating most of the foods that you enjoy and can lead you to a better lifestyle.

The Ketogenic diet is really a person dependent diet. It is meant so that you can engage in a healthy lifestyle by getting your body into Ketosis. As long as you follow our recipes and be consciously aware of your food input, you will feel an increase level of energy, and decrease in cravings, and most likely result in weight loss.

This diet is a great way to live, eat long term, and is easy to do. Remember that in order for this diet to be very effective, exercise is recommended.

Hopefully we have provided you with enough information for you to begin or continue your Ketogenic journey. All of the recipes in this book are Keto friendly. All you have to do is plan you meals in advance and you're well on your way. We hope that by reading this book, you have become more knowledgeable in determining the best diet for you.

Lastly, if you enjoyed this book, we look forward to you leaving a review on our Amazon page.

Thanks you and good luck!

Printed in Great Britain
by Amazon